D1237598

TROY POLAMALU

Kathleen Tracy

Mitchell Lane

PUBLISHERS

P.O. Box 196
Hockessin, Delaware 19707
Visit us on the web: www.mitchelllane.com
Comments? email us: mitchelllane@mitchelllane.com

Mitchell Lane
PUBLISHERS

Printing   1   2   3   4   5   6   7   8   9

A Robbie Reader Biography

Abigail Breslin	Drake Bell & Josh Peck	LeBron James
Adrian Peterson	Dr. Seuss	Mia Hamm
Albert Einstein	Dwayne "The Rock" Johnson	Miley Cyrus
Albert Pujols	Dwyane Wade	Miranda Cosgrove
Alex Rodriguez	Dylan & Cole Sprouse	Philo Farnsworth
Aly and AJ	Eli Manning	Raven-Symoné
AnnaSophia Robb	Emily Osment	Roy Halladay
Amanda Bynes	Emma Watson	Selena Gomez
Ashley Tisdale	Hilary Duff	Shaquille O'Neal
Brenda Song	Jaden Smith	Story of Harley-Davidson
Brittany Murphy	Jamie Lynn Spears	Sue Bird
Charles Schulz	Jennette McCurdy	Syd Hoff
Chris Johnson	Jesse McCartney	Taylor Lautner
Cliff Lee	Jimmie Johnson	Tiki Barber
Dakota Fanning	Johnny Gruelle	Tim Lincecum
Dale Earnhardt Jr.	Jonas Brothers	Tom Brady
David Archuleta	Jordin Sparks	Tony Hawk
Demi Lovato	Justin Beiber	**Troy Polamalu**
Donovan McNabb	Keke Palmer	Victoria Justice
	Larry Fitzgerald	

Library of Congress Cataloging-in-Publication Data
Tracy, Kathleen.
Troy Polamalu / by Kathleen Tracy.
  p. cm. — (A Robbie reader)
Includes bibliographical references and index.
ISBN 978-1-61228-059-2 (library bound)
1. Polamalu, Troy, 1981– —Juvenile literature. 2. Football players—United States—Biography—Juvenile literature. I. Title.
GV939.P65T73 2012
796.332092—dc23
[B]
                                                                2011016789

eBook ISBN: 9781612281711

ABOUT THE AUTHOR: Kathleen Tracy has been a journalist for over twenty years. Her writing has been featured in magazines including *The Toronto Star*'s "Star Week," *A&E Biography* magazine, *KidScreen*, and *TV Times*. She is also the author of over 85 books, including numerous books for Mitchell Lane, such as *The Fall of the Berlin Wall*; *Paul Cézanne*; *The Story of September 11, 2001*; *The Clinton View*; *We Visit Cuba*; *Megan Fox*; *Mariah Carey*; *Orianthi*; and *Kelly Clarkson*. Tracy lives in the Los Angeles area with her two dogs and an African gray parrot.

PUBLISHER'S NOTE: The following story has been thoroughly researched and to the best of our knowledge represents a true story. While every possible effort has been made to ensure accuracy, the publisher will not assume liability for damages caused by inaccuracies in the data, and makes no warranty on the accuracy of the information contained herein. This story has not been authorized or endorsed by Troy Polamalu.

TABLE OF CONTENTS

Chapter One
Belief 5

Chapter Two
Back to Nature 11

Chapter Three
Raw Talent 15

Chapter Four
Transformation 19

Chapter Five
Tasmanian Angel 23

Career Statistics 28
Chronology 29
Find Out More 30
    Books 30
    Works Consulted 30
    On the Internet 30
Glossary 31
Index 32

Words in **bold** type can be found in the glossary.

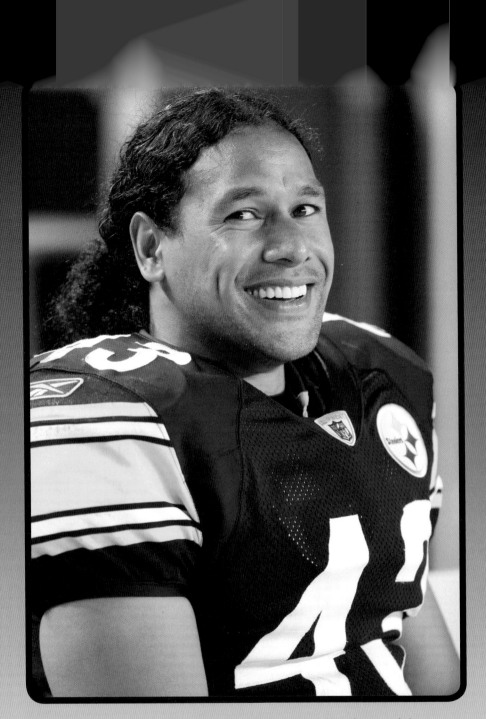

A hard hitter on the field, Troy Polamalu is considered one of the National Football League's true gentlemen off the field. His college roommate, Carson Palmer, says, "His heart off the field is just to be the greatest guy that ever was. Nice to everybody—great guy, great human being, respectful, humble, everything you could ask [for]."

Belief

It wasn't supposed to be like this. Troy Polamalu was used to being the best player on the football field. In high school he had been an award-winning athlete. In college, he was voted one of the top players in the country. He expected to have the same kind of success as a **professional** football player when the Pittsburgh Steelers drafted him in the first round. But in his **rookie** year, he hardly played. And the few chances he got, he played poorly.

His second year as a pro did not start out any better. Polamalu was frustrated and unhappy. He began to doubt himself.

"I really questioned my life and my manhood," he told *Pittsburgh Catholic* magazine.

In the third game of the season, the Steelers played the Cincinnati (sin-sin-AT-ee) Bengals. Troy's college roommate, Carson Palmer, was the Bengals **quarterback**. Palmer was leading his team down the field. They were close to scoring a **touchdown**. He passed the ball and Polamalu stepped in front of the **receiver** (ree-SEE-ver). The football was coming right at him.

"I had the ball in my hand and dropped it," he said. Had he caught the ball, he could have run for a touchdown. Instead of being a hero, Polamalu felt like a failure.

"I thought, 'Man, there went my chance to make everybody happy, to get all these doubters off of me.' I was so angry and frustrated that I started crying on the sidelines."

So he did what he always did when troubled. Polamalu prayed.

"I sat there with my head in my hands, crying as I was praying."

Then he noticed what song was playing on the stadium speakers. "It was Los Lonely Boys

Polamalu's first interception as a pro happened on October 3, 2004, in a game against the Cincinnati Bengals. On the Cincinnati team was receiver Chad Ochocinco (#85) and quarterback Carson Palmer, Troy's college roommate.

By early 2011, Polamalu had a total of 27 career interceptions and had run two back for touchdowns. He says he just goes with the flow of the game. "I know where I'm supposed to be at the time of the snap. Now, wherever the play dictates where I'm going to go is a different story."

singing, 'Lord, take me from this prison, I want to get away.' "

To Polamalu, it was a sign. He should not give up. He had to keep trying. If he stayed positive, good things would happen. "Just like that, I felt everything was going to be great."

Later that same game, Polamalu was again on the field playing **defense** (DEE-fents). There were less than two minutes to play. The Steelers led 21-17, but the Bengals had one more chance to win the game. Palmer took the snap and passed the ball—and this time Polamalu **intercepted** (in-ter-SEP-ted) it. He ran 26 yards for a touchdown to seal his team's win.

"You better believe I was on the ground, saying, 'Thank you, God, thank you!' " he said. "That's one of the many ways he has revealed himself to me."

On the field, Polamalu is a fierce **competitor** (kum-PEH-tih-tur). But off the field he is gentle and deeply religious. His journey from a troubled youth to role model shows the power that faith, and a loving family, can have.

Polamalu is almost as famous for his hair as he is his play. He views football as a kind of war and says his hair reflects that. "Throughout history, every great warrior—the Greeks, the Samurais, the American Indians, the Mongolians, you name it—had long hair and would dress it before battle."

Back to Nature

Troy Benjamin Aumua (ow-MOO-ah) was born on April 19, 1981. He is the youngest of five children. Both his father and his mother, Suila Polamalu (soo-EE-lah pah-luh-MAH-loo), are of Samoan descent. Samoa is an island in the South Pacific.

When Troy was a toddler, his parents divorced. Suila moved with her children to Fountain Valley, which is a half hour south of Los Angeles, California. When he got older, Troy stopped using his father's last name and began using his mother's.

A lot of gangs were in their neighborhood. All four of Troy's older siblings got into trouble with the law and spent time in jail. As a young boy, Troy also felt the pull of gang life. It seemed certain that he would also end up in jail one day.

In 1989, when Troy was eight years old, Suila took her kids on vacation to Tenmile, Oregon, to visit her brother Salu and other family members. Tenmile was a small community out in the country. Fewer than 600 people lived there, but many of them were Troy's relatives.

Troy had never seen a cow before. He also had never experienced so much open space. Instead of being surrounded by buildings, he was surrounded by nature. When it was time to go back to California, Troy told his mother he wanted to stay longer.

"I was only supposed to stay for three weeks," Troy said, according to a USC football web site. "But I fell in love with the place. It's beautiful. I called my mom and begged her to let me stay up there. I just knew I had to get away. She had maybe a split second to make the decision. My mom made a very brave decision. It must have hurt her a great deal, but she let me stay. She knew it was best."

Samoa, formerly known as Western Samoa, is located in Oceania, a region in the South Pacific about half way between Hawaii and New Zealand.

"He spent the summer," Salu told reporter Patrick McManamon, "and then he just stayed."

It was a choice that changed Troy's life forever.

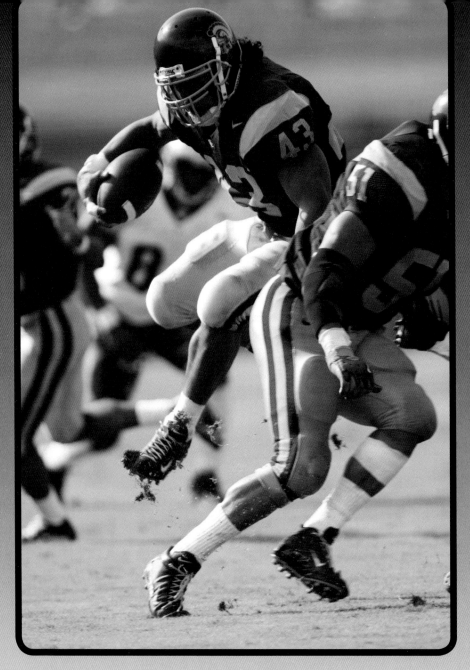

In his career at the University of Southern California as a three-year
starter, Polamalu amassed 278 tackles; six interceptions, three returned
for TDs; 13 deflections; two fumble recoveries; and four blocked punts.

Raw Talent

In the Samoan culture, children are often raised in large and extended families. Uncle Salu, who had come to the United States from Samoa in 1965, and his wife, Kelley, treated Troy as one of their own. Troy's other Oregon relatives embraced him as well.

"I was kind of raised by a community of people," Polamalu explained to the *Akron Beacon Journal.* "Not **helter-skelter** like; I've been very blessed. I had twelve aunts and uncles—six on my mother's side of the family— all of them have five or more children. My **generation** [jeh-neh-RAY-shun], my cousin, my brothers and sisters, is the first generation to be born in America."

Even as a young boy, Troy was athletic. But talent needs **discipline** to grow. And Troy admits he was a troublemaker as a boy.

"Problems follow you wherever you go," Polamalu told McManamon. "I think the turning point was the discipline my uncle showed in my life. Everybody may need it in a different way, but I needed it in a military boot camp way."

In college, Troy was close friends with his roommate, quarterback Carson Palmer. Today, Palmer considers his friend the best defensive player in the NFL. "Once he's on the football field . . . , his heart takes over. He's not going to let you complete a pass. He's going to smack you around, he's going to knock you out."

Troy entered Douglas High School in 1994, and sports became his passion. He played on the football, basketball, and baseball teams. For a while, it seemed he might become a professional baseball player. He batted .550 and was first-team All-State. But his heart was in football.

He played on both defense and **offense** (AH-fents) for his high school team. In 1996, Douglas High's football team was undefeated. Troy was named the league's Offensive Player of the Year. Even though he was not very big physically, he was an even better defensive player. He was fast, strong, and fearless.

During his senior year, Troy suffered a bruised kidney and a torn back muscle during a game. Even though he didn't play the rest of the season, many colleges offered him **scholarships** (SKAH-lur-ships). In the end, he agreed to enroll at the University of Southern California (USC).

After ten years in Oregon, it was time for Troy to go back home.

Polamalu is considered small for the NFL, but he makes up for his size with athleticism and brute strength. Teammates say he trains even harder than he plays. Polamalu believes, "Any time you can squeeze out the opportunity to get better, you should."

CHAPTER FOUR

Transformation

As expected, Polamalu became a star college football player. He also used college to learn more about his **heritage** (HAYR-ih-tij). He joined some **Polynesian** (pah-lih-NEE-zhun) groups and studied his native culture and language. He took a trip to American Samoa to experience his roots and to visit his mother. She had moved back to Samoa when Troy was in high school.

While in college, Polamalu began dating Theodora Holmes. She was the sister of his teammate Alex Holmes. Theodora says she and Polamalu fell in love quickly.

Polamalu ended his college career on a high note. USC went 11-2. After beating Iowa

38-7 in the **Orange Bowl**, they finished as the fourth-ranked team for the 2002 season.

The Pittsburgh Steelers chose Polamalu in the first round of the **draft**. It was the first time the Steelers used a first-round selection on a defensive **safety**. Although small for professional football at 5 feet 10 inches and 200 pounds, Polamalu had the strength of a much larger player.

Polamalu was excited to play professional football. Theodora moved to Pittsburgh to be with him. They got engaged in 2004 and were married in 2005.

Growing up in California, Polamalu had attended Catholic school. In Oregon, he had gone to Mormon and Protestant churches. He considered himself a Christian but did not follow a particular group until he met Theodora. She introduced him to the Greek Orthodox Church. On his days off from football, he and Theodora attend church together.

On Halloween in 2008, Troy and Theodora's first child was born. They named him Paisios (py-EE-see-ohs). Their second son,

Troy is a devoted family man and enjoys spending time with his children. "I take pride in my life—my wife, my family. I try my best not to have football define the person that I am."

Ephraim (eh-FRY-um), was born September 16, 2010.

Faith and family are Polamalu's top priorities. But he also enjoys being in the public eye. When a shampoo company asked him to be their **spokesman**, it was an offer he could not refuse.

Polamalu is in the 2011 Guinness World Records for having his hair insured for $1 million, the most insured in the world. His hair has made him a TV star in Head & Shoulders shampoo commercials. "I was blown away when they asked me to be in this new spot," he says.

Tasmanian Angel

It's easy to spot Troy Polamalu when he's on a football field. Billowing out from under his helmet is a long mane of hair. Stretched straight, it is over three feet long. Polamalu admits he goes years between haircuts. But it is not a fashion statement. He wears his hair long to honor his Samoan ancestors.

Procter & Gamble, the company that makes Head & Shoulders shampoo, hired Polamalu to star in some television commercials (kuh-MER-shuls). The commercials became so popular that Procter & Gamble insured Polamalu's hair for $1 million. Now he is almost as famous for his hair as he is for playing football.

Polamalu is using his **celebrity** (seh-LEH-brih-tee) status to help others. In 2007, he and Theodora founded the Harry Panos Fund. It is named in honor of her grandfather, who fought in World War II. The fund benefits injured soldiers.

Troy says he wants to be a good role model, now and in the future. "Being an

Polamalu won Super Bowl rings with the Pittsburgh Steelers in 2006 and 2009. While he enjoys being in his team's victory parades, he's uncomfortable with personal awards, such as when the Steelers voted him their MVP. "Football is such a perfect team sport, it's hard to make anybody a most valuable player."

In an impressive play against the Tennessee Titans in 2010, Polamalu leaped over the offensive and defensive lines to make the sack—before the quarterback could take a single step. "I just jumped," he recalled. "It was a blast."

athlete, you are automatically a role model," he said on USC's football web site. "But this will end one day, so I've always wanted to become a teacher."

To that end, Polamalu did something few professional athletes do: he returned to school. In the spring of 2011, NFL football players were not allowed to go to training camp. The owners and the players union could not agree on a new contract. The owners locked the players out.

Polamalu did not just sit around and worry about when, or if, the season would start. He spent his time letting an ankle injury heal. He also earned his college degree in history. He received his diploma with 1,000 other USC students on May 13, 2011.

"I'm officially a USC graduate!" he announced on his web site. "I decided to finish what I started and walked that stage today not only because it was very important to me personally, but because I want to emphasize the importance of education. . . . I truly love football . . . but it's certainly not a replacement for an education."

For as long as he's still playing, Polamalu will continue to play hard. "I have developed the Samoan mentality—you have to be a gentleman everywhere but on the field. On the field, play like it is a game of life. Give everything you have. If you go out and play things safe, you can end up getting hurt. So

I always try to lay myself out on the line and **sacrifice** [SAK-rih-fys] my body for the team."

He says he also plays to glorify God. "Football is part of my life but not life itself," he explained on the Mystagogy web site. "It's what I do; how I carry out my faith." Some opponents have nicknamed him the Tasmanian Devil, but he prefers a different nickname: the Tasmanian Angel.

In May 2011, Polamalu graduated from college, showing he has as much brain as he does brawn. "I don't think I have a split personality," he says. "I'm the same person at home—passionate about everything I do, whether it's reading the Bible or hanging out with my wife."

CAREER STATISTICS

Year	Team	G	TOT	SOLO	ASST	PD	SACK	FF	INT	YDS	TD
2003	PIT	16	38	30	8	4	2.0	1	0	0	0
2004	PIT	16	96	67	29	15	1.0	1	5	58	1
2005	PIT	16	91	73	18	8	3.0	1	2	42	0
2006	PIT	13	77	58	19	10	1	1	3	51	0
2007	PIT	11	58	45	13	9	0	3	0	0	0
2008	PIT	16	73	54	19	17	0	0	7	59	0
2009	PIT	5	20	18	2	7	0	0	3	17	0
2010	PIT	14	63	49	14	11	1	1	7	101	1
Career		107	516	394	122	81	8	8	27	328	2

(G=Games played, TOT=Total tackles, SOLO=Solo tackles, ASST=Assisted tackles, PD=Passes defended, SACK=Quarterback sacks, FF=Forced fumbles, INT=Interceptions, YDS=Yards on returns, TD=Touchdowns scored)

CHRONOLOGY

1981 Troy Benjamin Aumua is born on April 19 in Garden Grove, California. He will later change his last name to his mother's last name, Polamalu.

1989 Troy moves to Tenmile, Oregon, and lives with his uncle Salu and Aunt Kelley.

1994 He enters Douglas High School.

1996 Troy is named first team All-Far West League.

1997 He is named All-State high school player.

1998 Troy is named Super-Prep All-Northwest.

1999 Troy accepts a scholarship and enrolls at the University of Southern California (USC).

2002 He is named All-American at USC.

2003 He is drafted by the Pittsburgh Steelers before he can earn his degree.

2004 Troy and Theodora Holmes become engaged.

2005 Troy and Theodora are married.

2006 With the Pittsburgh Steelers, Polamalu wins his first Super Bowl on February 6.

2007 He converts to Greek Orthodox Christianity. Troy and Theodora establish the Harry Panos Fund to help wounded veterans.

2008 Their first son, Paisios, is born on October 31.

2009 With the Pittsburgh Steelers, Polamalu wins his second Super Bowl on February 1.

2010 Procter & Gamble, the makers of Head & Shoulders shampoos, insures his hair for $1 million. Troy and Theodora's second son, Ephraim, is born September 16.

2011 In the off-season, during the NFL lockout, Polamalu earns his college degree in history from USC.

FIND OUT MORE

Books

Sandler, Michael. *Troy Polamalu (Football Heroes Making a Difference)*. New York: Bearport Publishing, 2011.

Whiting, Jim. *Troy Polamalu (Superstars of Pro Football)*. Broomall, PA: Mason Crest Publishers, 2008.

Works Consulted

Cole, Jason. "Tuesday Conversation: Troy Polamalu." *Yahoo! Sports*, September 25, 2007. http://sports.yahoo.com/nfl/news?slug=jc-tuesdayconversation092507

Farrar, Doug. "Troy Polamalu Gets His College Degree." *Yahoo Sports*, May 14, 2011. http://sports.yahoo.com/nfl/blog/shutdown_corner/post/Troy-Polamalu-gets-his-college-degree?urn=nfl-wp2029

Hillier, Gina Mazza. "Troy Polamalu: Player with a Passion for Jesus." *Pittsburgh Catholic*, August 31, 2008. http://www.pittsburghcatholic.org/newsarticles_more.phtml?id=1746

McManamon, Patrick. "Mane Man For Steelers—Reserved Polamalu Demon on Defense." *Akron Beacon Journal*, February 3, 2006.

Mazza, Gina. "The Mane Man." *Pittsburgh Magazine*, August 2009. http://www.pittsburghmagazine.com/Pittsburgh-Magazine/August-2009/The-Mane-Man/

Mystagogy, The Weblog of John Sanidopoulos. "A Wild Interview With Troy Polamalu." August 8, 2009. http://www.johnsanidopoulos.com/2009/08/wild-interview-with-troy-polamalu.html

"NFL: Troy Polamalu's Wife Theodora." *BW*, June 8, 2009. http://ballerwives.com/2009/06/08/nfl-troy-polamalus-wife-theodora/

Paige, Woody. "Locks to Make Plays." *Denver Post*, January 27, 2009. http://www.denverpost.com/broncos/ci_11560102

USC Trojans Football—Player Profile: Troy Polamalu http://www.usctrojans.com/sports/m-footbl/mtt/polamalu_troy00.html

On the Internet

Facebook: Troy Polamalu
http://www.facebook.com/troy43

National Football League: "Troy Polamalu, DB of the Pittsburgh Steelers at NFL.com"
http://www.nfl.com/players/troypolamalu/profile?id=POL041872

The Official Web Site of Troy Polamalu
http://troy43.com/

GLOSSARY

celebrity (seh-LEB-rih-tee)—A famous person.

competitor (kum-PEH-tih-tur)—An opponent in a contest.

defense (DEE-fents)—In sports, the side that is trying to keep the other team from scoring.

discipline (DIH-sih-plin)—Self-control; sticking to a task.

draft—The choosing of college or amateur players to play for professional teams.

generation (jeh-neh-RAY-shun)—The people who are born and living around the same time.

helter-skelter—In a careless way.

heritage (HAYR-ih-tij)—Family background or culture.

intercept (IN-ter-sept)—In football, to catch a ball thrown by the other team.

offense (AH-fents)—In sports, the side that is trying to score.

Orange Bowl—A college football game held every year in Miami, Florida, played between top college teams.

Polynesian (pah-lih-NEE-zhun)—Coming from Polynesia, a region in the South Pacific.

professional (proh-FEH-shuh-nul)—Someone who earns a living in a specialized job.

quarterback (KWOR-ter-bak)—In football, the player who runs the offense by handing the ball off to a runner or passing the ball to a receiver.

receiver (ree-SEE-ver)—An offensive football player who specializes in catching the ball.

rookie (ROO-kee)—A first-year professional.

sacrifice (SAK-rih-fys)—To give up something in order to gain something else.

safety (SAYF-tee)—In football, a player who tries to keep receivers from catching the ball.

scholarship (SKAH-lur-ship)—Money given to a student to pay for school.

spokesman (SPOHKS-min)—A person paid to promote a product.

touchdown (TUTCH-down)—In football, a goal made by a player who catches or carries the ball into the opposite end zone; a score worth six points.

INDEX

Cincinnati Bengals   6, 7, 9
Douglas High School   17
Fountain Valley   11
gangs   11–12
Harry Panos Fund   24
Head & Shoulders   22, 23
Holmes, Theodora (wife)   19, 20, 21, 24, 27
Ochocinco, Chad   7
Orange Bowl   20
Palmer, Carson   4, 6, 7, 9
Pittsburgh Steelers   5, 6, 9, 20, 24
Polamalu, Ephraim (son)   21
Polamalu, Kelley (aunt)   15
Polamalu, Paisios (son)   21
Polamalu, Salu (uncle)   12, 13, 15, 16
Polamalu, Suila (mother)   11, 12, 15, 19
Polamalu, Troy
    awards   17, 24
    being a role model   24–25
    birth   11
    charitable work   24
    childhood   11–12

children   20–21
commercials   21
education   5, 17, 19–20, 25–27
extended family   15
faith   6, 7, 9, 26
hair   10, 21, 22, 23
injuries   17, 26
interceptions   7, 8, 9, 14
marriage   20
NFL draft   20
nickname   27
religion   20, 27
self-doubt   5–6, 9
siblings   11, 15
training   18
Procter & Gamble   23
Samoa   11, 13, 15, 19, 23, 26
Super Bowl   24
Tenmile, Oregon   12–13, 15, 17
Tennessee Titans   25
University of Southern California (USC)   14, 16, 17, 19